Sky Pony Press books may be purchased in bulk at special discounts for sales promotion, corporate gifts, fund-raising, or educational purposes. Special editions can also be created to specifications. For details, contact the Special Sales Department, Sky Pony Press, 307 West 36th Street, 11th Floor, New York, NY 10018 or info@skyhorsepublishing.com.

Sky Pony® is a registered trademark of Skyhorse Publishing, Inc.®, a Delaware corporation.

Visit our website at www.skyponypress.com.

10 9 8 7 6 5 4 3 2 1

Manufactured in China, February 2024
This product conforms to CPSIA 2008

Library of Congress Cataloging-in-Publication Data is available on file.

Original text written by Hélo-Ita
Cover design provided by Mango Jeunesse
US Edition jacket design by Kai Texel
US Edition edited by Nicole Frail

Print ISBN: 978-1-5107-7978-5
Ebook ISBN: 978-1-5107-7979-2

CRAFT WITH
NATURE

A KID'S GUIDE TO CREATING WITH
MATERIALS FROM THE GREAT OUTDOORS

Hélo-Ita

Translated by Grace McQuillan

SKYPONY PRESS · NEW YORK

CONTENTS

A Word from the Artist   p. 4
Tips and Tricks   p. 5
Tools and Materials   p. 6-7

PRESSED LEAF GREETING CARDS
p. 9

WILD CRITTERS
p. 15

LUMINOUS LETTERS
p. 21

GREEN TOPPERS
p. 27

KAWAII ANIMALS
p. 33

HANGING FISH
p. 39

TINY BOATS
p. 45

COZY LUMINARIES
p. 51

A Word from the Artist

Hi there! I'm an artist and creator who loves crafting, decorating, cooking, and traveling. To bring the stories I imagine to life, I draw, tinker, cook, take photographs, and write—sometimes all at once!—for magazines, books, and other creative outlets. I especially enjoy going on long nature walks and then making things out of whatever objects I find along the way. If you take the time to look around you, even the tiniest leaf or the smallest little twig has a story to tell. There's something to learn about life from everything we see, and I think that is an amazing thing. This way of looking at the world is what I try to share with other people through my books.

Now it's your turn to create your own stories and bring the spirit of nature into your home!

Hélo-Ita

TIPS AND TRICKS

EIGHT PROJECTS, EIGHT NATURE-INSPIRED CREATIONS!

In this book, you'll find ideas and instructions for making decorative, fun, and imaginative pieces using natural materials that are easy to find in any season. You don't have to live in the country or next to an ocean to get started! The next time you take a walk, no matter where you are, just look around, and I'm sure you'll spot some real treasures: a leaf, a blade of grass on a sidewalk, a shell brought back from vacation, a nutshell in the kitchen, or even a ray of sunshine. . . . Embracing the spirit of nature means marveling at what the Earth has to offer–in summer and in winter and in the seasons in-between–in all of its beauty and simplicity.

The projects I'll show you in this book only require a few steps, and I want you to know that you can adapt them to whatever you have on hand. The models in the photos are there to give you ideas and to guide you, but every creation is unique, and that's what makes them all so special! Depending on which project you're working on, you could replace a twig with a drawing, a fresh flower with a pressed flower or pinecone, cloth with paper, a shell with a pebble, and the list goes on. Trust your own inspiration!

BEFORE YOU GET STARTED, HERE'S A LITTLE ADVICE . . .

● Use your time outside to collect **little treasures** like fresh and dry leaves, twigs, eggshells, berries, seashells, and pebbles . . . Wash or dry them as needed (tree leaves, for instance, may need to spend several days between two sheets of newspaper or paper towel in a heavy book). This will allow you to build up your supply of craft materials.

● If the time of year is right, you can use **fresh leaves** for your projects (though they are more delicate). First, place them between two sheets of newspaper inside a heavy book for a few hours to flatten them. A layer of varnish glue will protect the leaves and help preserve their color, but it won't prevent them from turning brown over time. *Warning:* Always keep fresh leaves whole. If you cut them, the edges will darken and the end result won't be as pretty.

● I often use **glue guns** for crafting because they are so practical. The glue dries quickly on any surface and it doesn't get all over the place! You can pick one up in a hardware store or anywhere that sells art supplies. If you don't have one, a little sticky putty will work for most of these projects (it's a little less solid, but making adjustments will be easier). White glue takes longer to dry but is also effective.

● Instead of using **construction paper**, I prefer to paint my own sheets of watercolor paper. When I'm finished, I end up with softer, subtler colors–and I can get all of the colors I need using one piece of paper so I don't have to waste anything!

TOOLS

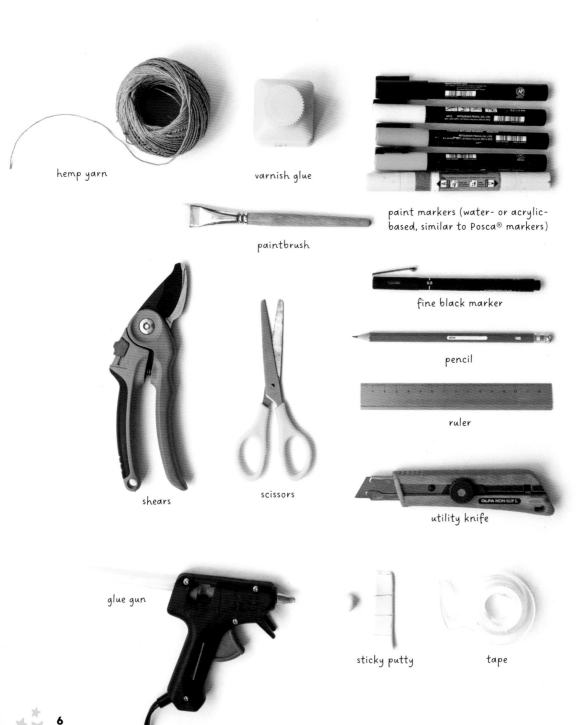

hemp yarn

varnish glue

paint markers (water- or acrylic-based, similar to Posca® markers)

paintbrush

fine black marker

pencil

ruler

shears

scissors

utility knife

glue gun

sticky putty

tape

MATERIALS

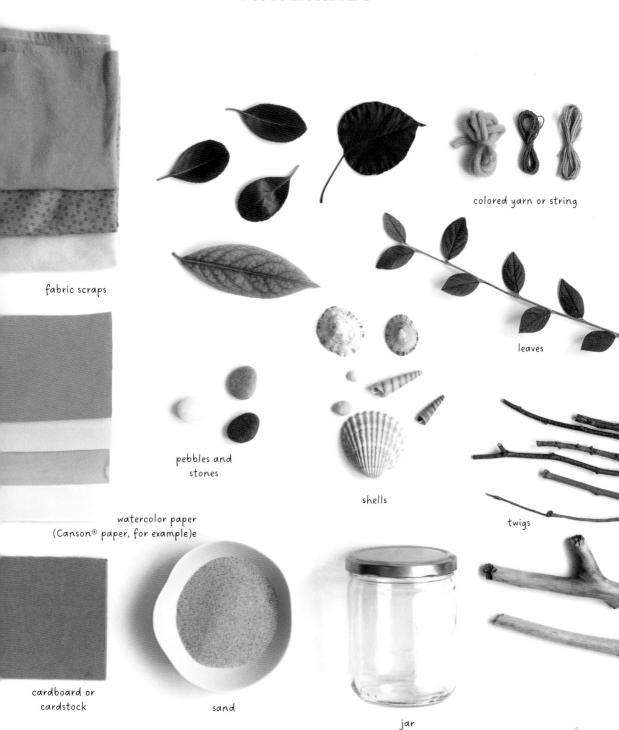

fabric scraps

colored yarn or string

leaves

pebbles and
stones

shells

watercolor paper
(Canson® paper, for example)e

twigs

cardboard or
cardstock

sand

jar

PRESSED LEAF GREETING CARDS

PRESSED LEAF GREETING CARDS

Here's how you can create personalized and pretty cards to send a kind word, holiday wishes, or a party invitation. If you want to, treat your leafy design like a work of art and frame it for a friend or to decorate your bedroom.

TOOLS

1 pencil

1 pair of scissors

1 glue gun (or strong glue)

1 sheet of newspaper (or paper towel)

Fine paint markers (water- or acrylic-based, like Posca® markers), 1 white and 1 black

MATERIALS

- 3 pairs of pressed leaves in 3 different sizes (1 large pair for the bodies, 1 medium-sized pair for the wings, 1 small set for the beaks)
- 4 very thin twigs or dried stems (for the legs)
- 1 sheet of white cardstock (watercolor or Canson® paper work, too) A5 size (5.82 x 8.26 inches, 14.8 x 21.0 cm)
- A few pieces of colored cardstock or painted paper

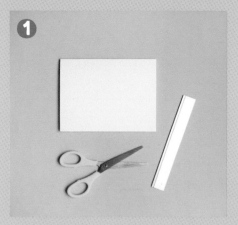

1

Cut a piece of cardstock to A5 size (see dimensions on p. 14 if your cardstock is a different size) and fold it in half lengthwise.

2

When you're happy with your design, take a photo or do a quick sketch of it to remember what it looks like.

Make two birds: use the biggest leaves for the bodies, the medium-sized ones for the wings, the small ones for the beaks, and the twigs for the legs.

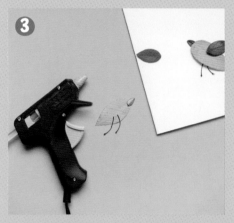

3

Turn each bird over onto the sheet of newspaper. Glue the smallest leaf to the back of the large leaf to form the beak (the pointy tip should stick out). Then glue on the twigs.

4

Glue the two little birds so they are facing each other, then glue on the medium-size leaves to make wings.

5

Draw circles with the white marker to give each bird an eye. Let dry, then use the black marker to draw the pupils.

6

Cut out a heart from a piece of colored paper and glue it between the 2 birds. Now all you have to do is write your message on the inside.

- If you don't have all of the items on the list of materials (twigs for the legs, a beak . . .), just draw them!
- To protect your leaves and keep them firm, apply a layer of matte or glossy varnish glue before you make your card. Either one is fine; what you choose depends on the look you're going for.
- If you want your creations to last a long time, use pressed leaves whenever possible.

WILD CRITTERS

WILD CRITTERS

I made this bird out of objects I collected on the beach one summer. You can build your own with whatever natural treasures you have around your house! And don't be afraid to mix things up—driftwood and seashells can be paired with pinecones and acorns for a wonderfully funny woodpecker!

TOOLS

1 glue gun

Sticky putty

1 gimlet

MATERIALS

- For the bird: natural and recycled materials (driftwood, seashells, frosted glass, small stones, etc.)
- For the base: a piece of wood, wooden skewer
- Acrylic paint

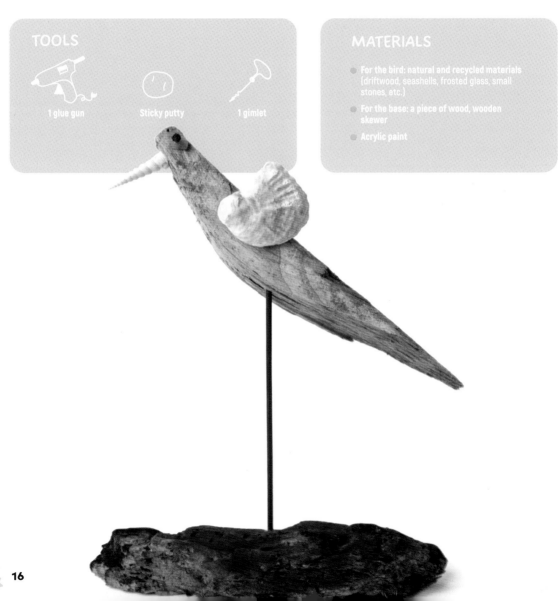

Choose any objects you want and design a bird, animal, or imaginary creature. Attach the pieces to each other with a little bit of sticky putty.

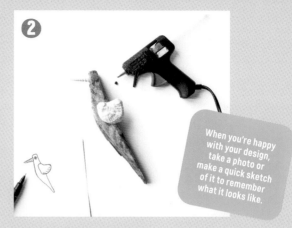

When you're happy with your design, take a photo or make a quick sketch of it to remember what it looks like.

Next, glue the objects together.

Prepare your base: choose a very stable piece of wood and drill a hole in the center (this is where you will attach the skewer*).

Put some glue on the end of the skewer and push it down into the hole.

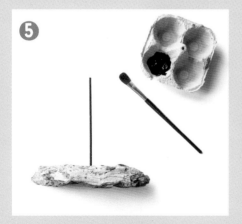

Paint the skewer and base black. Let dry.

Now drill a hole in the bottom of your animal sculpture with your gimlet. Press the sculpture onto the tip of the skewer.

* *Warning:* A gimlet should only be used under adult supervision!

LUMINOUS
LETTERS

LUMINOUS LETTERS

Why buy a decorative light when you can personalize your own?
Make one large letter or even a short word using individual branches (like I
did here for the "A") or bundle several thinner branches together and use
those. Living branches will be easier to manipulate and are less likely to break.

TOOLS

1 pair of
shears

1 pencil

1 glue gun

1 pair
of scissors

MATERIALS

- 1 sheet of A4 size paper [8.5 x 11 inches, 21 x 29.7 cm]
- A few branches (remove leaves and any pieces you don't need)
- Colored cotton string (or yarn, ribbon, silicone or art tape, etc.)
- Flowers and/or leaves, fresh or dried
- 1 string of LED lights

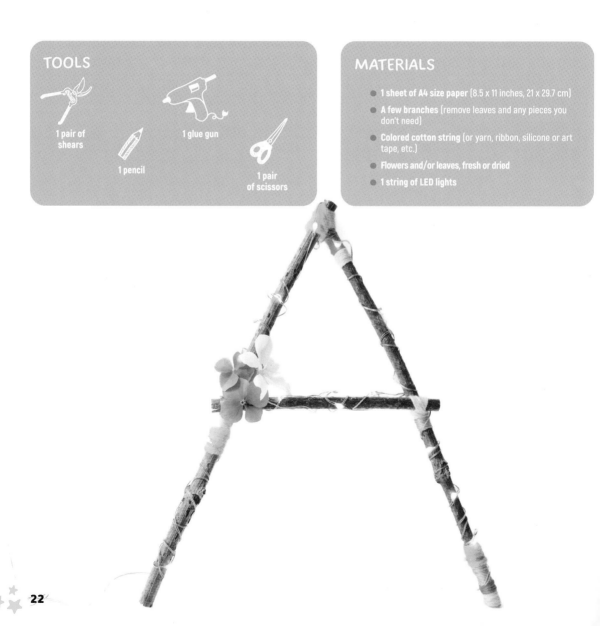

1

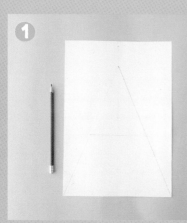

Trace your letter on a sheet of A4 paper. This template will tell you how many branches you will need and what size they should be.

2

Use the shears* to trim the branches to the right size. Arrange them on your sheet of paper and use a marker or pencil to mark where they need to be glued together.

3

Glue the branches together. Use your template to make sure they are positioned correctly.

4

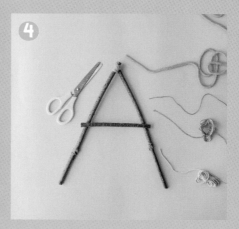

Reinforce your design by tying colored string around each junction. Add more glue if necessary.

5

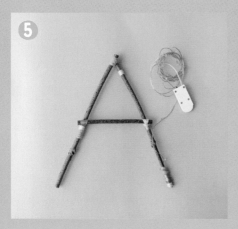

Wind your string of LED lights around the letter.

6

Add fresh flowers or other objects from nature for a rustic look.

*Warning: Shears should only be used under adult supervision!

23

- Soft, thin branches will work best if you're trying to make a round letter (ivy is an excellent choice and is relatively easy to find). Create your design and then trim one or several branches to the appropriate length. Bend them around a pot or jar with the diameter you're looking for to form the letters (like O, C, and U) or parts of a letter (the rounded parts of B or D) that you need. Hold everything in place with rubber bands. Let the branches dry and take on their rounded shape for at least 48 hours before using them.

- For a longer-lasting decoration, decorate your letter with pressed leaves or flowers.

GREEN TOPPERS

Whether you're hoping to brighten a birthday cake or create a fairyland in your own home, these plant decorations are just the thing! For the body of the butterfly, use a dried catkin (these spiky clusters of flowers can be found hanging from certain trees in the spring or fall and look like caterpillars). In the spring, wild grass seed heads are another beautiful option. If you don't have either of these, a small twig will do the job perfectly.

TOOLS

Varnish glue or liquid white glue

1 pencil

1 pair of scissors

1 paintbrush (to apply the glue)

1 paint marker (water- or acrylic-based, such as Posca® markers)

MATERIALS

TO MAKE A BUTTERFLY:

- **2 pairs of pressed leaves** (2 large leaves for the top wings, 2 smaller, longer leaves for the bottom wings)
- **1 tree catkin or small twig** (for the body of the butterfly)
- **1 thin branch 4 to 6 inches (10 to 15 cm) long,** as thick as a birthday candle
- **Cardstock** (like Canson® paper)
- **1 birthday candle holder** (or some aluminum foil)

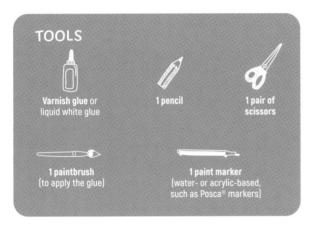

1 Choose two large, pressed leaves for the butterfly's top wings and two longer and smaller leaves for the lower wings. Cut off the leaf stems.

2 Fold a square of cardstock in half. It should be big enough to hold your butterfly. Arrange the leaves on either side of the fold, then trace a rough outline of your butterfly with a pencil so you know where to glue the leaves.

3 Paint the backs of the small leaves with glue, and glue them down on either side of the fold. Do the same with the larger leaves. Press down and flatten the leaves.

4 Coat the tops of the leaves with glue. Extend your layer of glue onto the paper around the leaves. This will help them stick better and protect them from light. Let dry.

Add decorative designs to the wings with a paint marker.

Now cut out your butterfly, following the outline of the leaves. Glue a tree catkin on top of the fold for the body.

Trim your branch if needed. Cut out a small circle of paper, make a hole in the center, and push the base of your branch through the hole. Place the branch in the birthday candle holder.

Gently bend your butterfly so the wings are not completely flat. Then glue it to the top of your branch. Now it's ready to grace the top of a delicious birthday cake!

> TIPS <

- Leaves that have been pressed flat will be easier to glue and will adhere better to the paper.
- Before gluing on the body of your butterfly in step 6, place the cutout of your butterfly between two sheets of parchment paper in a heavy book for a few hours. This will keep the leaves from curling.
- You can make your butterfly even more realistic by gluing on small seeds for eyes and twigs for antennae.
- If you don't have a birthday candle holder, you can place your toppers directly in the cake. Just wrap a little aluminum foil around the bottom of your branch to keep things hygienic.

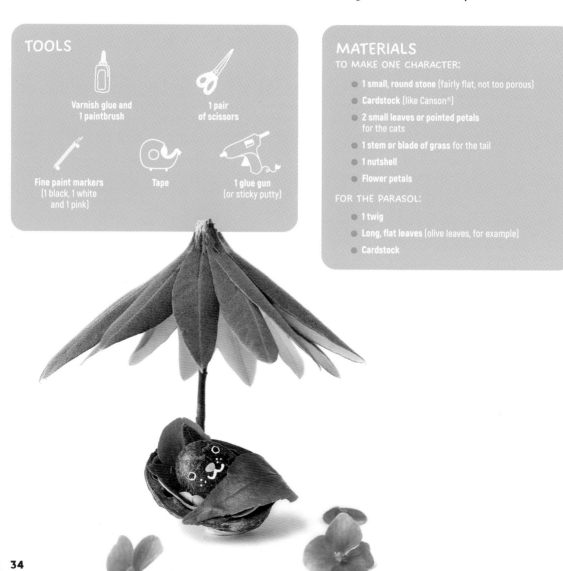

KAWAII ANIMALS

With nothing but a few stones and some markers, you can bring your own animal menagerie to life! Play with different ear shapes to create your real or imaginary animals: pointy leaves, round petals, twigs, berries, seeds . . . anything works. Then it's time to build beds, furniture, and accessories for your kawaii animals (kawaii means "cute" in Japanese, by the way). It's up to you to fill this adorable miniature world with whatever you can dream up!

TOOLS

Varnish glue and
1 paintbrush

1 pair
of scissors

Fine paint markers
(1 black, 1 white
and 1 pink)

Tape

1 glue gun
(or sticky putty)

MATERIALS

TO MAKE ONE CHARACTER:

- **1 small, round stone** (fairly flat, not too porous)
- **Cardstock** (like Canson®)
- **2 small leaves or pointed petals** for the cats
- **1 stem or blade of grass** for the tail
- **1 nutshell**
- **Flower petals**

FOR THE PARASOL:

- **1 twig**
- **Long, flat leaves** (olive leaves, for example)
- **Cardstock**

Paint a layer of varnish on the stone and let dry.

Draw the eyes, snout, and whiskers with the paint markers. Let dry between each layer of paint.

Glue the leaves onto cardstock. Paint them with varnish and let dry. Cut out the leaves and leave a little bit of extra paper at the base of each ear.

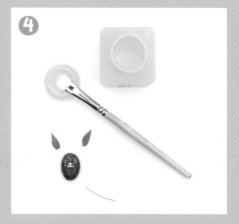

Glue the ears to the back of the stone along with a blade of grass for the tail.

Now it's time to make a cozy nest. Arrange a few flower petals inside a nutshell, and once your character is ready for bed, tuck it in with another petal or a leaf.

35

1 Take your cardstock and cut out a 2-inch (5 cm) circle. You can use a compass or small jar to trace the circle before cutting it out.

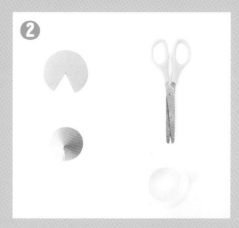

2 Starting from the center of your circle, cut out a triangle (like you're cutting a slice of cake). Roll the rest of the circle into a cone and attach the sides with tape.

3 Put a drop of glue on the tip of the cone and attach one leaf. Do the same with a second leaf, allowing it to slightly overlap with the first one. Keep going until the cone is covered.

4 Put one large drop of glue inside the cone and attach a twig that's around 4 inches (10 cm) long for the pole.

⇒ TIPS ⇐

- Put one large drop of glue inside the cone and attach a twig that's around 4 inches (10 cm) long for the pole.
- If you can't find all of these materials in nature, here are a few alternatives: to make the ears, replace the leaves with pieces of paper, replace flower petals with a fabric scrap for the blanket, or use a matchbox for the bed instead of a nutshell.

HANGING
FISH

HANGING FISH

These decorations won't last as long if you use fresh leaves instead of dried ones, but they'll still be just as pretty. The fresh leaves will be easier to work with if you let them flatten for a few hours between two heavy books.

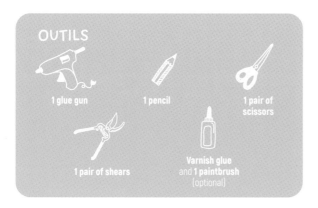

OUTILS

1 glue gun

1 pencil

1 pair of scissors

1 pair of shears

Varnish glue and 1 paintbrush (optional)

MATERIALS

- A few thin branches that are curved or flexible (like ivy)
- Leaves (for the scales)
- 1 olive, berry, or small fruit pit (for the eye)
- Cardboard or cardstock
- Twine or string

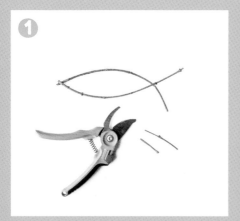

Choose two slightly curved branches and cut them* so that you're left with two long pieces of the same length as well as two short pieces (the short pieces are for the tip of the tail and the head).

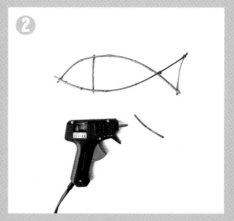

Design your fish, then glue the branches together.

Wrap twine around each junction to reinforce and decorate your fish. You can glue the ends to the back of the fish to hold them in place.

Place your fish on a piece of cardboard, then trace and cut out the shape of your fish's body and tail.

* *Warning:* Shears should only be used under adult supervision.

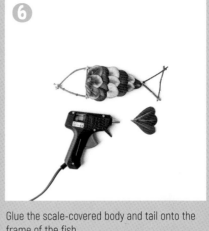

Now you can begin layering and gluing your leaves to cover the cardboard, starting with the tail. When you reach the head, cut off any leaves that stick out (if using dried leaves) or bend and glue them under the cardboard (if using fresh leaves).

Glue the scale-covered body and tail onto the frame of the fish.

Glue or tie a small pit (in this picture, I used a dried olive) to a piece of twine and attach it to the top of your frame to make the fish's eye.

To help the leaves stay shiny and to hold them in place, paint with a layer of varnish glue and let dry.

TIP

You can hang as many fish on the wall as you like or assemble several fish and make a mobile. If you choose the second option, plan to glue a second set of leaf-covered cardboard pieces (steps 4, 5, 6) to the back of the frame so the fish look fabulous on both sides.

TINY
BOATS

TINY BOATS

Give this project a try, and you'll feel like you're on vacation in your own home all year long! Even when summer is far away, and even if you don't have any sand or seashells on hand, you can still build these little boats—just replace the sand with a little bit of fine semolina flour or polenta and use a small piece of wood or a pebble instead of a seashell. It will look just as cute either way!

TOOLS

1 glue gun   1 pair of shears   1 pair of scissors

MATERIALS

FOR THE BOAT:
- 1 empty glass jar with lid
- Fabric/paper scraps
- 1 seashell
- Small twigs
- Sand
- Twine
- Cardstock
- Transparent fishing line (or fine, light-colored thread)
- Rubber band

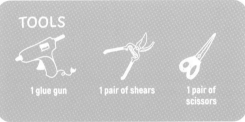

1 Cut out two small right triangles from your fabric scraps. One should be slightly larger than the other, but make sure that when you line them up next to each other, the total length is roughly equal to the length of the shell that will form the hull of your boat.

2 Trim two twigs* so you have one piece for the mast and another to reinforce the bottom of the larger sail. First glue a piece of twig to the bottom of your large sail and then glue everything to the mast.

3 Place a large drop of glue in the bottom of the seashell and attach the mast. Glue another piece of twig to the shell for the prow.

4 Run a length of twine from the top of the mast to the seashell and another down to the prow of your boat (you can either tie a knot or use a little glue).

5 Cut out a small fabric triangle and glue it to the twine to make a flag.

6 Pour a little sand into the bottom of the jar, then delicately place your boat inside.

Cut two small birds out of a sheet of cardstock and glue them to the ends of two pieces of fishing line.

Glue the fishing line to the inside of the lid. Make sure the two lines are at different heights and not too close to the center of the lid. Once the lid is turned over, the birds should look like they're floating in the air. Adjust the length of the lines as needed.

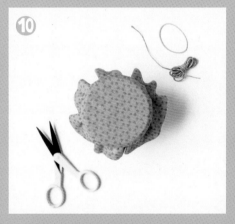

Cut out a circle of fabric that is around 1 inch (a few centimeters) wider than your lid.

Screw the lid onto the jar and place the rubber band around the cloth so it doesn't slide (you can also use a dot of glue to attach the cloth to the lid). Then tie some twine around the lid as decoration.

COZY
LUMINARIES

COZY LUMINARIES

If you're looking for a way to bring a touch of nature and whimsy to a holiday dinner table or a shelf in your home, then use this project to build a village in the clouds! You can build several houses of different sizes, then connect them with adorable little ladders or bridges made out of twigs. For even more magic, light up your village with LED candles.

TOOLS

Tape

1 utility knife and **1 cutting board**

1 pair of scissors

1 fine black marker, several colored markers or pencils

1 glue gun (or sticky putty)

MATERIALS

- **1 conical shell** (like a Chinese hat snail shell)
- **1 LED votive candle**
- **1 small twig** (preferably with berries or leaves)
- **White cardstock** (thick but not too thick, as light needs to be able to pass through, so 80 lb (120 gsm) is perfect)
- **1 sheet of colored cardstock or cardboard**
- **Loose lambswool, cotton balls, or kapok** (this is often used to stuff cushions) for the clouds

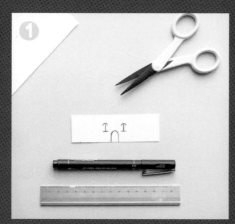

Cut out a 1 x 4-inch (2 x 10-cm) strip of paper. Draw a door in the middle and a capital "I" on each side to make the windows.

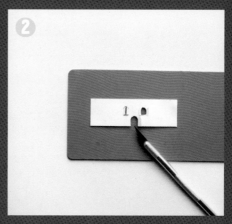

Use a utility knife* to cut out the door (leave it attached on one side) and the windows. Follow the lines you drew.

Open the door and shutters. Color the parts that are visible, then draw on details with the fine marker.

Form a cylinder with the strip of paper and attach the ends with tape or a little glue.

Apply some glue or sticky putty to the inside of the shell and attach it to your paper cylinder.

Using your colored cardstock, draw and cut out a pear shape that is a little larger than your candle.

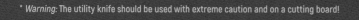

* *Warning:* The utility knife should be used with extreme caution and on a cutting board!

53

Make two small Xs with the utility knife. Later, this is where you'll attach the flame of your LED candle and the twig.

Gently press the flame of your LED candle and the twig through the cardstock base.

To make sure your twig tree stays in place, glue a ball of sticky putty under the cardstock at the base of its trunk. The piece of twig below the paper base should not be longer than your candle. Trim if necessary.

Glue the wool or cotton all around the paper base to make a cloud and hide the candle. Now you can set up your house!

> **TIPS** ≈
- Fill your village with houses of all different sizes! Varying the shape and number of windows is a great idea, too.
- For a country-style cloud village, you can replace the wool with moss.